J
612.662
MAH
Mahoney
Now you've got your period.

now

you've

got your

period

Ellen Voelckers Mahoney

THE ROSEN PUBLISHING GROUP, INC./NEW YORK

To my mother,
Barbara Walters Voelckers

Published in 1988 by The Rosen Publishing Group, Inc.
29 East 21st Street, New York, NY 10010

Copyright 1988 by Ellen Voelckers Mahoney

First Edition

Library of Congress Cataloging in Publication Data

Mahoney, Ellen Voelckers, 1952 —
    Now you've got your period.

    Bibliography: p.
    Includes index.
    Summary: Discusses the physical and emotional aspects of getting one's menstrual period. Also explains what happens during a pelvic exam.
    1. Adolescent girls — Health and hygiene. 2. Menarche. 3. Menstruation. [1. Menstruation]
    I. Title.
RJ144.M34 1988   612'.662   8-3223
ISBN 0-8239-0792-9
                                    12.95

Manufactured in the United States of America

A B O U T   T H E   A U T H O R ◇

Originally from New York, Ellen Voelckers Mahoney is a writer now living in California with her husband, Kevin, and her cat, Kelly. She is also the author of *Food for Fitness and Sports*. She wrote this book to help young girls be better prepared and have an easier time with their periods and growing up than she did. Ellen has a Master's Degree in Education from the University of Southern California and is especially devoted to writing about health-care subjects.

ABOUT THE ARTIST ◇

Born in Caracas, Venezuela, Nancy Anne Diem is a freelance illustrator who has worked in New York City and Los Angeles. Now living in California, Nancy is a graduate of the Art Center College of Design.

Contents

Foreword

When I was a teenager my mother gave me a box of Kotex and said, "Here, you'll be needing these soon." That was my total introduction to menstruation and puberty.

From talking to teenage patients now in my practice, I don't think things have progressed much further.

Why couldn't such a book have been available then—a book that explained how other girls felt; a book that told me how to pronounce the words that described the parts of my body that suddenly seemed new and strange.

I applaud this book, and I know it will save young girls from fear of the unknown and make this experience the remarkable passage to a full and healthy life that it really is.

Jane D. Patterson, M.D.

Dr. Patterson is the author of *Woman Doctor: The Education of Jane Patterson, M.D.* and, with Lynda Madaras, *Womancare: A Gynecological Guide to Your Body.*

CHAPTER 1

What Makes You So Special?

No matter how many ways men and women become alike in family roles and careers, women will always be unique in their ability to conceive and bear children. Although childbirth could not happen without men, bearing children is a woman's role. That is what makes you different and special. It's amazing to realize that for many, many years you will be able to reproduce, whether or not you choose to do so. In addition to such factors as your personality, your health, your looks, and your upbringing, your possession of a reproductive cycle is one of the most important parts of who you are. Naturally, a basic part of all this is your menstrual periods.

Each and every young woman begins and continues to have her periods in her own individual way.

Anne

"I guess you could say I was a late bloomer. All my girl friends had already begun to have their periods by

the time we were in eighth grade. I remember I used to feel pretty jealous that I didn't have mine yet. When I finally did in the ninth grade, I was happy even though my stomach hurt a lot."

Laura

"My mom had already told me about menstruation, and we saw a film in school that sort of prepared me. But I wasn't prepared for how my younger brother acted. When he found out I got my period, he kidded me about it all the time. It was embarrassing."

Jennifer

"For two months before I actually got my period, I had this funny brown discharge that would last a few days. My mother told me I was beginning my period. It was surprising because I thought I was going to really bleed a lot at first."

Nicole

"I have an older sister, and when I got my period I already knew about it from talking with her. The day it finally came, my mom and sister gave me a very pretty nightgown. I felt strange inside. Good. Like I was suddenly growing up."

SO MANY DIFFERENT REACTIONS

Every day we go through lots of changes, and for the most part the people around us are constantly making comments and reacting to us. As an adolescent you are experiencing all sorts of changes, and they are being noticed. Both your body and your mind are maturing. When something important happens—like getting your period—people are going to react.

Kevin

"For a long time my next-door neighbor Lisa was one of my best friends. We grew up together. I'll never forget the day she got her period. We were supposed to go to the shopping center together, but when I phoned her she wouldn't go. After I bugged her to tell me what was wrong, and I found out it was her period, I just decided to leave her alone. The thing is, she thought it would bother me, but it didn't bother me at all."

Sarah

"My family was vacationing one summer in Florida. I was having a good time, except that my younger sister and I seemed to be fighting over every little thing. All of a sudden she became very nervous because she realized she had just gotten her period for the first time. I showed her how to use a sanitary pad and then we talked a long time about growing up. It turned out to be a good day for both of us."

It's wonderful to realize what great strides women are making in their overall contributions to our world. Women have more opportunities now, more choices, and I think they have gained a new kind of respect. In general, there is greater acceptance of the feminine features that make a woman a woman. This, naturally, includes menstruation. However, the acceptance of menstruation was not always easy or positive.

In the past many taboos and folk tales surrounded a young woman having her period. Some of those beliefs were indeed ridiculous.

- In Persia a menstruating woman was thought to be possessed by an evil demon. After giving birth to a girl child, a woman was obliged to lie in front of a hot fire for fourteen days to cleanse herself.
- In Egypt a woman was slapped across the face if she complained of cramps.
- In Rome a menstruating woman was believed to destroy entire crops, wilting plants if she merely walked by them.
- In East Africa anything a menstruating woman touched was considered poisoned. To eat her meals

she had to crouch in a dark corner by herself, eat, and then throw away or burn her dishes.

- In South Australia a man who walked by a menstruating woman would be considered contaminated. The woman had to warn a passerby that she was having her period. If a man was not warned and happened to walk by such a woman, it was believed that he would weaken and suddenly grow old.
- In Alaska Indian women of the Dene tribe had to wear a hat called a "menstrual bonnet" and a thick veil to cover their face during their periods.
- In California in 1988 coworkers, friends, and even family members giggle and make jokes when they find out I'm writing a book about menstruation. Some of their jokes even make me laugh!

It's certainly no secret that even today people have some very peculiar attitudes about menstruation. Although these attitudes are changing, we still have a long way to go before we stop thinking of menstruation as unclean or unmentionable. To be honest, I still have a few negative feelings about getting my period that are hard to let go of. Sometimes I feel unattractive, angry, or clumsy during this time. It's easy to feel frustrated if my face breaks out or if I put on a little weight. Often I feel especially vulnerable, and usually I feel tired for a day or two. But I don't regard my period as a "curse," even though it can be annoying. It's really discouraging when people say things like, "She's in a bad mood because she's 'on the rag'." Such remarks and attitudes only make women feel less confident, and they put down the very person we are—a woman. Having a positive attitude about menstruation and understanding as much as you can about your body and yourself will surely bring you greater happiness in life than a negative outlook and misinformation.

MORE THAN ANYTHING ELSE

This book is intended to help you feel better about yourself by answering many of the questions you may have about menstruation and growing up. I wish I had asked for help when my first period came, because it was a difficult time. Part of the trouble was that I wasn't prepared and didn't turn to anyone for guidance. I had terrible cramps, I had trouble using pads, and my period seemed to come all the time. My life had taken a miserable turn! Now I realize that many things could have been done to make myself feel and look a lot better. These are the things I want to share with you now. So get ready for basic information about your developing body, your menstrual cycle, PMS, hormones and emotions, reproduction, dealing with menstrual and related discomforts, seeing a doctor, being healthy, and keeping a calendar.

In addition to reading this book, don't hesitate to talk with people who can offer advice and reassurance. Many people around you can help—your mom, one of her friends, your dad, your sister, a good friend, a teacher, a school nurse, grandparents, a health practitioner, or a doctor. Nobody said growing up was easy, but more often than not talking with others can help solve the confusions and worries that are only natural.

CHAPTER 2

Your Changing Looks and Body

Valery

"Being thirteen wasn't easy. Being fourteen was even harder. I remember I was one of the tallest girls in the class. That wasn't so bad, I guess, except that I was a little chunky around the middle. I had long thin legs, and my younger sisters teased me that I looked like a pickle barrel on toothpicks. My hair was oily, and my skin was always breaking out. Fortunately I liked to sew, so it was great when I could make myself new clothes that were in style. But when I looked at the beautiful models in *Seventeen* magazine sometimes I just wanted to crawl under my bed and hide."

Wanting to be attractive and to fit in and be accepted by your friends and classmates is a natural and positive thing. But most of us, like Valery, are at some time or another unhappy with our looks, whether it's the style of our hair, our weight, our complexion, our height, or the size of our nose or our ears. If we chose to do so, we could make a list of complaints about our bodies that would be endless. On the other hand, our list of things we like about ourselves could also go on and on. It's an individual decision.

Susan

"Sometimes I just hate listening to my friend complain about her big nose. All she talks about is having a nose job, and probably some day she will. I have a reddish birthmark on my cheek. I use makeup to cover it, but really there is nothing I can do to get rid of it. It's not as if I can have surgery, and it's frustrating to know I'll always have a mark on my face. But one time Mom told me that a birthmark is an angel's kiss. I know it's a silly thing that isn't true, but when she said that it made me feel so much better. Every time I start to get down on myself about my red mark, I think, 'It's an angel's kiss,' and then it's not so bad. Nobody's perfect. . .I still think I'm pretty."

For many young women growing into adulthood can be an awkward time. Hormonal changes are going on inside that can cause unpleasant changes on the outside such as oily skin and hair.

Brette

"Every time I get rid of one pimple, two more show up! I hate it! I hate having rotten skin. My dermatologist says my skin will clear up with the right medication and time. But I don't care about looking good in high school. I want to look good now."

It can be very difficult in today's world to feel happy with our looks. Wherever we go we constantly see magazines, TV shows, feature films, and billboards with pictures of beautiful women and young girls. We look at these images as perfect, and sometimes we think we also must look and be perfect. But we're not. Nobody is.

When you see a beautiful brown-eyed brunette or blue-eyed blonde staring at you from the cover of *Mademoiselle* or *Teen Magazine*, realize that the model was one out of thousands of candidates who competed for the coveted covergirl position. And remember that the gorgeous covergirl has had great makeup and excellent photography to make her look her best. Given the right ingredients, it's my guess that most of us could look like covergirls—if we wanted to.

The next time you stand in front of a mirror and find fault with your features and your looks, remember one thing. When you grow older and have a business career or get married, you are not going to keep that job or that marriage because of your looks. Your looks may get you in the company door or across the threshold, but they won't keep you there. Looks cannot guarantee success. Intelligence, a positive attitude, a high energy level, strength, and a willingness to work hard can and will.

Everyone has something remarkable about her, whether it's a smile, beautiful hands, unusual eyes, or wavy hair. Whatever it is, there is always something. Be happy with yourself, and others will feel positive about you too. Think for a moment, and then write down ten or more things you really like about your looks. Then write down ten or more things you really like about your personality.

PUBERTY

For the .most part, growth and change are gradual processes. But puberty, the time when young people begin to develop into young adults, can be quite abrupt. You may suddenly notice all sorts of changes about yourself that require getting used to. Although everyone develops at an individual rate, certain typical female changes take place during puberty.

- Your height increases and levels off at your full height.
- Your breasts develop and increase in size.
- Pubic hair grows around your genital area.
- The hair on your legs thickens, and hair grows under your arms.

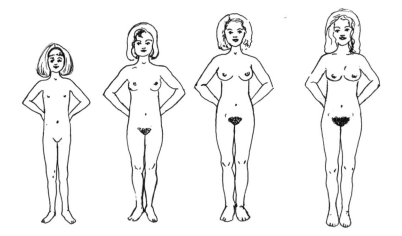

Changes in Puberty. As you become a woman, your body goes through many noticeable changes.

- Your hips widen and your body becomes more curvaceous.
- Your uterus and vagina grow.
- Menstruation begins.
- Your skin and hair probably become oilier.
- You begin to perspire more.
- Romantic sexual feelings will become more apparent.

You look like a woman, but you feel like a girl.

Jessica

"I just turned ten, but I already wear a B-cup bra. Next year I'll probably wear a C. I'm not ready to look like my older sister, who's fifteen. I still like my stuffed animals and I still like playing outside. Am I supposed to be all grown up just because I look like a woman? I'm not ready."

Some girls like Jessica begin to develop quite young. Their breasts develop, they get their period before other girls do, and pubic hair begins to show. This is normal.

It's important to remember that the changes you experience during puberty are just *beginning* changes toward your becoming a woman. In many ways becoming a woman is a slow process, and it is dependent on having new life experiences and taking on new responsibilities. It's okay to feel like a girl when you are young like Jessica. You still *are* a girl. Someday you will have matured physically and emotionally, and you will be a woman.

SKIN

Having clear, smooth skin is wonderful, but when you're a teen it is more often the exception, not the rule. During puberty your hormones are working overtime and stimulating the oil glands of your face and scalp. The result is often acne. Blackheads, whiteheads, cysts, and pimples appear on the face, the back, the shoulders, and sometimes even on the scalp.

Nobody wants to have pimples, and even a mild breakout can be annoying and frustrating. Because there is an increase in the male hormone androgen just before your period begins, skin problems are usually worse at that time.

The first step in combating acne is to see a dermatol-

ogist, a specialist in the treatment of skin problems. All sorts of topical and oral medicines are available that seem to have positive results. Each person has to figure out what works best for her.

In addition to seeing a skin doctor, you yourself can take many preventive measures to ensure clear, clean skin. Wash your face frequently with a soap designed to help problem skin, or the clear brown-colored bars. Ask your doctor or a facialist to recommend a soap that will help and not irritate your skin. You may wish to use an alcohol astringent after washing to tighten the pores; however, astringents can have a drying effect. Next apply a benzoyl peroxide product to help heal existing blemishes.

Try to keep your hands away from your face, because hands carry many germs. When you talk on the phone, don't rest the mouthpiece against your chin; it's another great source of germs. Although some dermatologists disagree, I think it's important to avoid (as much as you can) the following foods when your skin is breaking out:

Chocolate
Cola and carbonated beverages
Milk products
Coffee
Buttery/greasy foods

Too many sweets tend to have a negative effect on one's health and skin. Plenty of exercise, at least eight hours of sleep each night, and drinking plenty of water will help your skin tone. You may wish to see a skin facialist every once in a while for a more thorough cleansing than you can do at home.

Last, if you use makeup buy products that are allergy-tested or designed for problem skin. It's a good idea to use a water-based foundation, because oil-based ones can aggravate acne.

HEIGHT AND WEIGHT

Alexandria

"I dread going to the doctor because I hate having to
be weighed. I know I need to lose weight, and when
you're at the doctor's the real truth about your weight
comes out."

Most young girls don't worry much about their weight or
what they eat until they reach puberty. Puberty is an important time of self-realization when we want to "look
good" for our friends of the same and the opposite sex. But
puberty is often a time when weight seems to go up rather
than down and when girls grow quite a bit taller than guys.

Since you were about two you've grown about two
inches a year. In puberty your growth rate can double,
taking you from a height of, say, 5'1" to 5'5" in just one
year. Usually after your first period this growth spurt will
level off, and you will continue to grow one or two inches a
year until you reach your full height. Boys go through this
growth spurt a few years later than girls, and most boys
eventually become taller than girls. But, naturally, this is
not always the case.

Bones grow at different rates during puberty, and your
feet often reach adult size years before you reach your
adult height. So you may be on the short side but have
seemingly large feet. With time your body will catch up
and seem to "grow into" your foot size.

You will also notice during this time that you gain fatty
tissue in your breasts, hips, thighs, stomach, upper arms,

and shoulders. Even your face grows longer and fuller during puberty. This normal weight gain is just that— normal. Some young girls, however, put on or lose too much weight during adolescence. Most people have weight fluctuations during a lifetime, but one's basic frame and stature can't be changed no matter what you do or don't eat. Right now you may be too thin or too heavy. Some- times it takes young people years to grow into an eating pattern with which they are comfortable. But once that happens, a person's weight can stabilize at a comfortable, attractive level. Some adults, unfortunately, never seem to reach this comfort level and are always on some diet or exercise program to take off or put on weight.

Realistically, almost all of us can control our weight and our lives so that we eat when we need to eat, have occa- sional snacks, and maintain good health. That is the ideal. I remember that during my teens I seemed to be famished all the time and was too often a compulsive eater. I didn't like this habit, but it was hard to break. I did change my eating patterns, however, and now I am happy with my medium to thin weight that rarely changes even though I eat three meals a day.

BREASTS

Even though it makes no difference *physically* (in the ability to reproduce) whether you develop earlier or later, it does matter *personally* to most girls. Breast development is often a big concern in adolescence. Maybe you think your breasts are too small or too large. Maybe you think boys would like you better if you had larger breasts. Maybe you think it's better to have smaller breasts that don't inter- fere with sports. Maybe you wish your nipples were dif- ferent. The fact is that breasts, like people, come in all shapes and sizes. Although large-breasted women are often portrayed in advertising as objects of sexual admiration, it's important to realize that *most* girls and women are not "stacked"—and they will find a boyfriend and a man to love and marry regardless of their breast size.

HAIR

Margo

"I'll never forget how happy I was when my mother finally let me shave my underarms and legs. I was nervous that I'd cut myself, but I used Dad's shaving cream and took my time. When I finished, my legs felt smooth as silk!"

During puberty new hair grows in the genital area and under the arms, and the hair on the legs thickens. Getting new hair can be dramatic.

Beth

"I was shocked—no, make that embarrassed. Somehow my older brother found out I had grown some pubic hair. Well, he teased me about it. But the day he told his friend Scott about it—I just about died!"

Growing hair in new places can be both exciting and disconcerting. For the first time in your life you really can see yourself becoming an adult. This can be scary, but fun. Because plenty of jokes are made about girls' genital areas, it can also be embarrassing to be the target of teasing. But boy are also growing hair and growing up, too.

CHAPTER 3

Your Body—Inside and Out

As you mature, it's easy to notice some of the changes happening on the outside of your body— your breasts grow, you get taller, your complexion changes, new hair begins to appear. All these changes are the result of fascinating transformations going on inside you. These are obviously difficult or impossible to see, but they affect your life and the way you feel. The more you know about what is happening inside you as you grow into a woman, the more you will be able to understand and *appreciate* who you are.

You have sex organs both inside and outside your body. The outer sex organs are called the *genitals* or *genital organs*. Both men and women have genitals. In a woman, these organs are sometimes called the *vulva*.

As the various organs are discussed in this chapter, you may wish to hold a mirror between your legs for a closer look at your body. Although every woman has the same genital organs, each person's body is slightly different, in the same way that each person's face is unique. When you

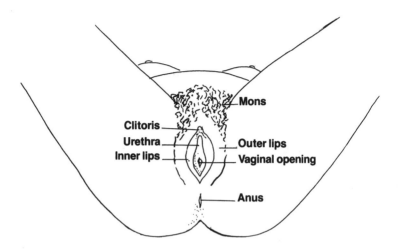

Female Genitals.

look at the diagrams in this book, remember that they will never look exactly like you. But they can give you a good idea of the shapes of body parts and where they are located.

THE MONS (monz)

At the top of the vulva is the *mons*, which is essentially a pad of fatty tissue that covers the pubic area and pubic bone. Pubic hair begins to grow on the mons during adolescence and then fills out in adulthood.

THE OUTER LIPS

As you look at yourself, you can see that the mons divides into two distinct folds of skin. These are the *outer lips*, or *labia majora*, a Latin term that means "major lips." These lips are soft and fleshy and are designed to protect the small openings in this area. Hair also grows to some extent on these lips for protection against outside air, germs, and infection.

THE INNER LIPS

By separating the outer lips you can see the *inner lips*, or *labia minora*, meaning "smaller lips." During childhood these inner folds of skin may not be noticeable. In puberty they take on a more definite form. Like the outer lips, their function is to protect and keep clean the genital area.

THE CLITORIS (CLIT-or-is)

The *clitoris* is a small budlike organ at the top and inside of where the inner lips join together. If you spread apart these lips, you can see the clitoris as a round bump of soft skin. This organ contains many nerve endings; it is a central site of sexual feelings and of the good sensation called *orgasm*.

THE URETHRA (u-REE-thra)

The *urethra* or urinary opening is located straight down from the clitoris. This is where urine is passed from the bladder to the outside. It is not easy to see the urethra because it is a very tiny opening.

THE VAGINAL OPENING (VAJ-in-al)

Directly down from the urethra is the *vaginal opening*, the opening to the passageway to the internal reproductive organs. During childhood this opening is very small. As you grow into adulthood the vaginal opening enlarges and becomes more apparent.

THE HYMEN (HI-men)

In some girls a thin layer of skin called the *hymen* lies across the vaginal opening. In slang the hymen is called the "cherry." Although not all young women have a hymen, most have some skin stretching across the vaginal opening, and some have a rather thick layer. Of course, the hymen has an opening to allow fluids such as menstrual blood to pass out of the body. In some cases the hymen is broken as a result of physical activity. Any stretching movement such as doing the split, slipping and having your legs fly out underneath you, or tumbling can stretch or tear the hymen. But having a hymen, not having a hymen, or having a torn hymen is no indication of whether a woman has had sex with a man or not.

THE ANUS (AIN-us)

The *anus* is not a sex organ, but it is located in the genital area. It is the opening through which solid wastes leave the body. The skin around the anus, like the skin of the inner lips, may change color during puberty and become slightly darker. Hair may also grow around the anus during puberty.

The sex organs inside the body are called the *reproductive organs* because they are essential to the ability to reproduce and bear children. It is difficult to say exactly when a girl becomes a woman, because from the time we are born our bodies begin to develop. But as you grow older, your sex organs grow larger and also change positions.

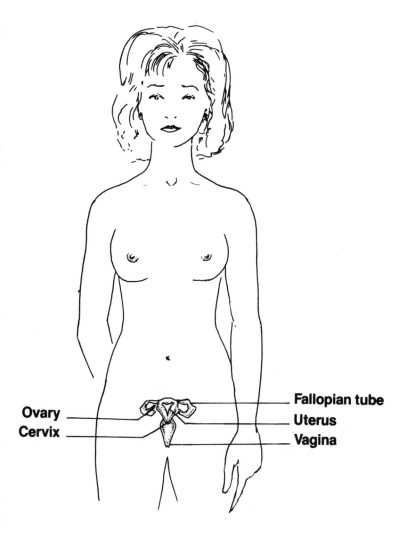

Ovary
Cervix

Fallopian tube
Uterus
Vagina

Female Reproductive Organs.

THE VAGINA (va-JI-na)

The *vagina* is the passageway that leads from the inside to the outside of a woman's body. Although the diagram depicts the vagina as tubelike, it is really more like an expandable pouch or balloon. In an adult woman the vagina is usually only about four or five inches long, yet it can expand enough to allow an entire baby to pass through from the uterus during childbirth. Most of the time, however, the vagina is like a popped balloon and its walls touch each other. If you put a (washed) finger in your vagina you can feel these soft, squishy walls. For some young women inserting a finger is difficult because the vaginal opening is too small or tight. If it hurts to do this, wait until you are older and your body has matured a bit more.

Menstrual blood passes out of a woman's body through the vagina, and a man's penis is inserted in the vagina during sexual intercourse to enable conception and reproduction.

THE CERVIX (SER-vix)

If you insert your middle finger into your vagina as far as it will go, you will be able to touch a smooth bump that feels like the tip of a nose. This is your *cervix*, which is at the very top of your vagina and the lower part of your uterus (womb). You may be surprised to discover how close your womb is to your genital area.

Like the vagina, the cervix grows during puberty. It is one to two inches in diameter in an adult woman. If you are able to touch your cervix, you may be able to feel a tiny depression in the center. This depression is the opening called the *os*, where blood leaves the uterus and where sperm passes into the uterus. The os is no bigger than the tip of a match, but this small opening can enlarge enough to allow a baby to pass through. It is important to know, however, that normally the os is tightly closed, and a finger or a tampon cannot go through it. Nothing that is inserted into your vagina can enter the rest of your body except sperm and, in the rare case, germs. To avoid infection, keep your vaginal area clean and wash your hands before inserting a finger inside. In the case of sperm, you *always* need to use birth control measures during sexual intercourse when pregnancy is not desired.

THE UTERUS (YOUT-e-rus)

The medical name for the womb is *uterus*. It is an organ about the size of your fist and the shape of an upside-down pear. Made up of thick walls of strong, stretchy muscle, the uterus is a remarkable organ designed to shelter and help develop the beginning of a new life. Once menstruation begins, the uterus is prepared to nourish a baby every month. The uterine lining is shed every month if fertilization has not taken place.

FALLOPIAN TUBES (fa-LOH-pee-an)

Two *fallopian tubes* extend from the top of the uterus, one on each side. These tubes are about four inches long and very narrow (about the width of a fine needle). Each of the fallopian tubes bends around one of the two ovaries. The outer end of each tube has fingerlike extensions that play an important role in conception. These extensions, called *fimbria*, reach out around the ovaries but do not touch them.

THE OVARIES (OV-a-reez)

About the size and shape of unshelled almonds, the two *ovaries* lie on either side of the uterus, close to the fallopian tubes. When you were born your ovaries contained about 400,000 eggs each. The eggs are called *ova*; one egg is called an *ovum*. As you mature and begin to menstruate, the ovaries release one ripened egg a month.

In addition to containing all the eggs you'll ever need to bear children, the ovaries have another important function. They make the vital female hormones estrogen and progesterone, which are chemicals that travel through the bloodstream and are responsible for many of the bodily changes during puberty. They are discussed further in Chapter V.

Individually, your reproductive organs—the vagina, the uterus, the fallopian tubes, and the ovaries—are incredible, intricate, and important parts of you. It is easier to understand how each functions, however, by understanding how all work together as a team during menstruation and reproduction.

CHAPTER 4

Reproduction

Because you are a female, your mind and body enable you to someday become a mother. You have the ability to give birth to a baby—to become its parent. That does not mean, however, that "motherhood" is your only purpose in life. It also does not mean that you should or must become a mother. It merely means that you are able to reproduce—if and when you want to.

Simply stated, reproduction means to make new again or to bring to life. Parents reproduce when they have children, and reproduction is nature's way of continuing life on earth.

Reproduction can occur when a man and woman want to have a child and are prepared to care for and love that young person. Reproduction can also occur even if a man and woman do not want to have a child. The ability to reproduce a new life is an exciting and rewarding experience *if* a couple want to and are ready to create that person. It is best and most intelligent, however, for couples to have children when they are both emotionally and physically ready. This is an important point, because you can be physically ready to have a child when you are young and not yet emotionally ready.

Most young women are physically ready to have a baby the moment they begin to menstruate. In other words, if you get your period when you are eleven, you could have a baby. A young man is ready to have sex and help create a baby the moment he begins to expel sperm from his body during puberty. Emotionally, however, young people are not ready to deal with the responsibilities of child-birth. This emotional maturity is reached much later in life.

To conceive a child, two important ingredients are needed: one egg from a woman's body and sperm from a man's body. The egg and sperm might be thought of as seeds. As for size, an egg is about the size of the period at the end of this sentence. Sperm are so small that they cannot be seen with the naked eye.

The reproductive cycle in a woman's body begins during puberty when one ripened egg bursts from one of her ovaries in the process called *ovulation*, a term derived from the word *ovum*. Ovulation occurs once every month, gen-erally in the middle of the menstrual cycle. For example, if your period started on November 1, ovulation would occur around November 14 and your period would begin again around December 1 (unless fertilization had occurred). If your period started on November 14, ovulation would occur around November 28 and your period would begin again around December 14. These dates are not exact and are used only to give you an idea of the time involved. Every female has a different menstrual cycle, and ovula-tion, like menstruation, can occur at *different times.*

You should remember, however, that whenever ovula-tion does occur, it is the time when you can become pregnant if you have sex.

"So I can just figure when it's okay to have sex without getting pregnant by counting back fourteen days from my period. Am I safe then?"

NO. The timing of ovulation is not an exact science. If you are having irregular periods, as many young girls do, your ovulation will occur at different times. You can never just count back a certain number of days in your cycle and think that these are "safe" days to have sex. One of my best married friends got pregnant just after her period ended. Sometimes our bodies just "do their own thing."

Not getting pregnant means not having sex or, if you do have sex, using birth control measures. And sometimes birth control doesn't keep you from getting pregnant.

As mentioned, you were born with approximately 400,000 eggs in each ovary, for a total of about 800,000 eggs. This is an extraordinarily large number considering that you will release only about 500 in a normal reproductive span from about thirteen to fifty years of age.

When the egg bursts out of the ovary, the fringe of the fallopian tube called *fimbria* reaches out like delicate fingers to catch the egg. The fimbria then draws the egg into the fallopian tube, where tiny hairs push it along so that it will be in a good position to meet and unite with the sperm.

If a man and women have sexual intercourse during the time when the egg is in the fallopian tube, it is highly probable that the egg from the woman and sperm from the man will meet in the tube. If this happens, a sperm breaks through the outer shell of the egg and moves inside it. This is *fertilization*, the joining together of egg and sperm to begin a new life.

Most of the time, however, the egg makes its way down the fallopian tube without meeting a sperm. In this case, the egg continues to the uterus, where it will be passed out of the body during menstruation.

If the egg has been fertilized, however, it attaches itself to the wall of the uterus, which has been preparing for a new life by building up a warm, nourishing lining. Then, for the next nine months, a baby develops.

As we have said, girls are born with thousands of eggs. Interestingly, boys do not have any sperm when they are born but produce sperm during puberty. This is a basic difference between boys and girls.

Sperm are made in the *testicles*, which are two oval-shaped organs in the man's *scrotum*. The scrotum is a soft sac of skin just beneath the *penis*. It is purposely located outside the body rather than inside, to keep the sperm cool. If the sperm were stored inside, the body heat would kill them and reproduction would not be possible.

In order for the egg and sperm to unite, sperm must leave the male's body and enter the female's body. This is called *sexual intercourse* and occurs when a man's penis enters a woman's vagina.

The penis, made up of spongy tissue, has two basic functions: to enable the man to urinate and to enable the man to help create a child. A tube called the *urethra* (the same term used for the woman's organ) runs down the inside of the penis. When a male urinates, the urine flows out of his body through the urethra. Sperm also travel through the urethra and are expelled when a man ejaculates. Because of the way a man's bladder is designed, it is impossible for urine and sperm to pass through at the same time.

A man's penis can enter a woman's vagina when he has an *erection*. When a man or a boy has an erection, blood rushes into the penis and fills up the spongy tissue. Then muscles at the base of the penis contract so that the blood remains in the penis and makes it hard. When the penis is

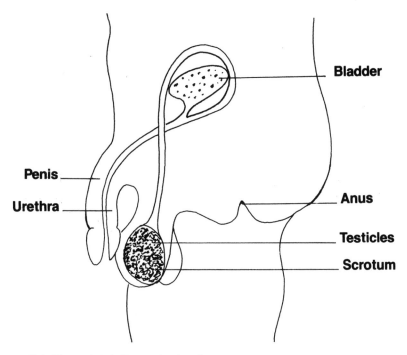

Side View of Male Reproductive Organs.

erect, it is longer and larger and stands out from the body. The hardness and the direction of the penis enable it to fit snugly into the woman's vagina.

A man's erection can recede of itself in time. The muscles at the base of the penis relax and blood flows out of the organ. The erection also recedes after the man ejaculates during sexual intercourse, masturbation (voluntary stimulation of the penis to produce orgasm), or a wet dream (involuntary ejaculation occurring during sleep).

Sometimes an erection is called a "boner" or a "hard-on" because it feels stiff as if a bone were inside, but there is no bone in the penis.

Throughout a male's life he can have erections—even in infancy. Rubbing or touching the penis or thinking sexy thoughts can cause an erection. And sometimes males have erections for no apparent reason—they just happen.

I remember my ninth grade biology class when I used to sit beside this guy I thought was pretty good-looking. He was athletic and seemed to be more physically mature than the other boys. But what I really remember is my surprise and confusion when I looked over at him and saw that he had an erection in his tight jeans. Although I knew some basic information about erections, I couldn't understand why he had one in the middle of class, and I just thought he was weird. Naturally, I later learned that it was a perfectly normal occurrence for a perfectly normal guy.

Now, back to reproduction. In order for sperm to leave a man's body and enter a woman's body, *ejaculation* must occur. This is a process by which sperm are released when the muscles of the erect penis contract and force the sperm up and out through the urethra. The sperm that leave the body are mixed in a creamy, whitish liquid called *semen*. In total, the secretion equals about an ounce of liquid, although it may be less or more. Semen contains millions of microscopic sperm. This is nature's way of trying to ensure fertilization, so that when sexual intercourse occurs during a woman's ovulation there is a greater chance that one sperm out of millions will unite with the egg. Ejaculation occurs simultaneously with the good sensation of orgasm.

After the sperm are ejaculated from the penis, they start swimming upward to the top of the vagina and pass through the cervix into the uterus. Not all the sperm make it that far. Some just drift back down the vagina or the uterus and dribble out of a woman's body with the rest of the semen.

Let's review some of the main points about reproduction.

What is ovulation? Ovulation is the monthly process whereby one ripe egg is released from an ovary so that fertilization may occur. In general, ovulation takes place two weeks (14 days) after the first day of the menstrual period. The following chart shows hypothetical examples of when ovulation would occur, based on a monthly menstrual cycle of 28 days.

	FIRST day of bleeding	ADD 14 days after bleeding starts	APPROXI-MATE day of ovulation
Kim	November 3	+ 14 Days	November 17
Melanie	November 10	+ 14 Days	November 24
Erica	November 25	+ 14 Days	December 8
Denise	December 5	+ 14 Days	December 19

Ovulation is the time when a female can become pregnant. In the chart, for example, the women could become pregnant respectively on November 17 and 24 and December 8 and 19.

Many females have irregular menstrual cycles, meaning that ovulation might occur at varying times. Bodies can be quite systematic, but they don't always operate like clockwork.

It is often difficult to tell when you are ovulating. But for some females a slight discomfort in the lower abdomen and a small amount of blood (a spot of blood on the underwear) may indicate ovulation.

What is fertilization? Fertilization is the meeting and uniting of a ripened egg of a female with a sperm of a male.

How is the egg fertilized? When a girl enters puberty, ovulation begins to occur. If she has sexual intercourse during ovulation, there is a good chance that fertilization will occur. Fertilization can happen the first time a female has sexual intercourse.

What is a sperm?   When a boy matures during puberty, millions of microscopic sperm begin to form in his testicles. These sperm are needed for fertilization and reproduction. Sperm leave the male's body through his sexual organ, the penis, in the fluid called semen.

Why must the sperm leave the male's body?   A baby is conceived when a sperm meets and unites with an egg. For this to happen, the sperm must reach the egg inside the female. To leave the male's body, sperm are released from his penis during ejaculation.

What is ejaculation?   The word *ejaculation* means to throw out or release. When a male ejaculates, millions of sperm are released through his penis. The sperm must leave the male's body to meet, unite with, and fertilize the female egg. It takes just one sperm to fertilize a female egg.

How do sperm enter a female's body?   The penis is shaped to fit comfortably in the female's vagina. This entry of penis into vagina is called sexual intercourse. The male's penis is able to enter the female's body when it becomes erect. During intercourse, the man and woman unite so that the egg and the sperm have the possibility of uniting. Intercourse usually happens when a man and woman feel love and sexual attraction for each other.

What if the egg is not fertilized?   Every month after a girl has begun menstruating, a ripened egg heads toward her uterus, the organ that has been preparing to nourish a new life. A female has the potential of conceiving every month.

If her egg does not meet and connect with a sperm, menstruation takes place.

How do you become pregnant? If you have sexual intercourse you can get pregnant, even it's your first time. For a few days every month, you produce a ripe egg that breaks out of your ovary and goes into your fallopian tube. If you have sex at this time and if (1) you use no birth control, (2) your birth control doesn't work, or (3) semen from the man's penis gets close to the lips of your vagina and sperm swim up through your vagina and uterus to your fallopian tube, there is a great chance you will become pregnant. Your egg will be penetrated by a sperm and fertilization (pregnancy) will occur.

How can you tell if you are pregnant? If you have had sexual intercourse and (1) you miss a period, (2) your period is late, or (3) your period is different from normal and your breasts hurt and you feel tired, go to someone like a parent or an adult you feel comfortable with for advice. Or go immediately to a health clinic or a doctor. Worrying that you might be pregnant can be a very scary feeling, and you must go to people who can and want to help you.

When are you ready for sex? The decision to have sexual intercourse is one of the biggest decisions of your life. If you are not prepared to handle the possible consequence of having a baby, it can be one of the *worst* decisions of your life.

In school and with your friends it can seem as though there's great peer pressure to have sex. It may sound as if "everybody's doing it," but most often the truth is, "everybody's just talking about it."

Remember that having sex cannot do things like give you

a prettier face, make you thinner, or give you a better personality. But having sex *can* give you a baby.

Can sex make you sick?   Yes. Sexually transmitted diseases (STD) such as herpes, gonorrhea, syphilis, and AIDS (acquired immune deficiency syndrome) can lead to severe illness and possibly death. Just remember that saying no to sex is not only okay, but it's *safe*. Deciding to have sex means carefully choosing your partner (someone who is a virgin, someone who has not slept around, someone who does not use drugs) and using condoms. Condoms are excellent for two reasons—they can prevent both pregnancy and STD.

CHAPTER 5

Menstruation

So far, we have discussed many important things relating to that exciting, strange, mysterious, and even hard-to-say word, *menstruation*. You've read about changes your body goes through during puberty. You've learned about important body parts that are changing, and you know more about the incredible process of reproduction. So where does menstruation fit in?

The word menstruation (MEN-stru-WAY-shun) comes from the Latin word *mensis*, meaning month. Every month, once your periods start, your body becomes completely involved in preparing to have a baby. That is pretty amazing when you stop to think about it. Every month your uterus begins building up a fresh lining of tissue and blood to nourish a tiny baby that might begin to grow. Usually, however, the uterine lining is not needed (you don't become pregnant), and it is discharged out of the uterus through the cervix and vagina to the vaginal opening. And now you've got your period. After your period has ended, your uterus will once again begin to develop a new lining—and on and on this monthly cycle goes.

GETTING YOUR PERIOD

With the exception of women who are pregnant, women who are nursing a baby, or women who have a physical health problem, all women have periods. Usually, young women begin their periods between the ages of nine and sixteen, and they continue to menstruate until they are about fifty.

No one girl starts her periods just like another girl. Everyone has a different reaction and feels different about starting menstruation. Some young women are delighted while others are depressed. Everybody is different, but one thing is certain: Getting a period is an important event in a young woman's life.

I remember the first time I ever heard about menstruation. My mom told me about it one day, and that night I lay in bed and tried to imagine what in the world she was talking about. Blood? Monthly cycle? What? I had trouble falling asleep, and I thought, "I am never going to do that—not me!" I had a strange feeling in my stomach, and I wished I had never heard about this new thing.

For the next few years I learned more and more about menstruation from school, my friends, and books. So by the time my first period came I felt okay about it. My mom gave me a sanitary napkin and belt and helped me put it on. I remember how bulky the pad felt. I also remember feeling a sense of importance inside—although I never told anyone.

WHEN AND HOW WILL IT START?

There is no exact way to know when you will first begin to menstruate, but it will happen when your body is ready. Most girls start about two years after their breasts begin to develop and about one year after their pubic hair begins to grow. Some girls begin to menstruate about the age their mother did.

My best friend in elementary school and junior high started her periods two whole years before I did. She also wore a bra and had pubic hair before me. I used to look at her in awe, thinking, Gee, you sure are mature for your age. And I always used to feel inside that I wasn't ready to be as mature as she was—yet. I wasn't feeling ready for puberty and getting my period.

I definitely thought, however, that when my first period came a lot of bright red blood would gush out of me, because that's what happens when you get a cut—blood runs out of it.

Periods are different, especially "beginning" periods, and many girls begin their menstrual cycle without even knowing it.

First of all, a whitish discharge may begin to appear in your underwear. This can happen for months before the discharge turns to a brownish color. Slowly, your body is maturing. And then one day you will discover some reddish blood in your underwear or on your toilet paper. Your period has arrived.

Marcia

"Don't ask me why, but I kept waiting and waiting for my period to come. My older sister had hers, and I thought it was cool. Like I said, don't ask me why— just kidding. So we went to see a movie and I went to the bathroom and saw this brown-colored stuff in my underwear. I was sure *that* wasn't my period. But the next morning "Charlie" came because there was red blood in my pajamas. My sister and I always called our

periods "Charlie." Anyway, I was real happy about the whole thing."

When you have your first period, it's not always easy to know when it will come again. It will become easier to know when to expect it as you get older. Usually you will be able to tell by feeling a wetness in your underwear, but there are recognizable signs:

- You may have a queasy stomach or cramps or both.
- Your breasts may swell and become tender.
- Your face may break out.
- You may feel more emotional.
- Your hair may become oilier.
- You may perspire more.
- You may feel bloated or gain weight because of water retention.
- You may feel tense and irritable.
- Your teeth and gums may be sensitive.
- You may feel more hungry and thirsty.
- You will find a little blood in your underwear or on your toilet paper when you go to the bathroom.

Many girls have light blood flow in their first periods. But it is still an understandable concern about when it will come. You worry that it might start in the middle of class or in a situation where it would be difficult to get to a bathroom. Sometimes this does happen, but by being aware of your body's signals you can tell just about when your period will start. As time goes on, you can also keep track of your monthly cycle so that you have an idea of the day it will begin. It's always a good idea to have a sanitary pad or tampon in your purse or locker or at home—just in case.

YOUR MONTHLY CYCLE

From the first day of bleeding of one period to the first day of bleeding of the next period usually is about one month, or 28 days on average. Some girls are very regular and get their period about the same time every month, but the menstrual cycle may be anywhere from 21 to 35 days.

The first year I menstruated I was very regular and it was great. But the second year I started to get my period every three weeks (21 days) and it seemed like every two weeks. I remember having bad cramps and finally going to the doctor. I was told that everything was okay and that in time my menstrual cycle would become regular again. To my relief, it did.

Many women, and especially young women who've just started having their periods, have irregular monthly cycles. In my case, like other young women, I think my body was just adjusting to the change of menstruation. But, again, having irregular periods seems quite "regular" for many young women. No two women have exactly the same cycle. You may have one, two, three, or all twelve periods the first year you start. On the other hand you may have two periods, skip two periods, and then start again.

Each woman has her own pattern, and no one is exactly sure why menstrual periods fluctuate and why some women are regular while others are not. It's not unusual for a woman to be regular all her life and then suddenly become irregular. But we do know that in menstruation lots of differences are considered normal.

Sometimes things such as excitement, stress, not eating right, illness, a change of environment, or a sudden weight change can alter your regular cycle. It's not uncommon for young women in their first year of college to completely skip their periods. A lot changes when a person goes to college—it's a new environment, it can be stressful, many exciting things happen, one's eating habits may change, and so on.

Ideally, however, a woman should have her periods. I've always felt better when my periods are on a normal schedule. If you do have a problem missing periods, it's a good idea to see your doctor and make sure you're okay.

WHAT ABOUT THE BLOOD?

You will probably lose only a small amount of blood the first time your period comes. At first it will have a brownish color, and then it will become more red. From time to time I've gotten the impression that guys and some girls think a woman loses about a cup or more of blood during a period. Picture an entire cup of blood! Some people also think that women become weak from losing a lot of blood during their periods. For the most part, this is not true.

Although it may seem that a lot of blood comes out during menstruation, it really isn't that much. For most women the amount of blood that is released during a period is about six tablespoons. Some women have heavier periods with about eight tablespoons of blood, whereas others have light periods and only one tablespoon. Some women have a pattern of alternating heavy and light periods.

Another question related to menstruation is, "Does the blood come out all at once?" Mostly, the menstrual blood dribbles out slowly over about five days. However, a period may last as few as two days or as many as eight days. Every once in a while you may feel more blood passing out, especially if you use sanitary pads.

The discharge that leaves your body during your period is actually made up of blood, uterine lining, and vaginal and cervical mucus. Usually the menstrual flow is heaviest the first few days and then tapers off. The color of the blood may change throughout the period from a brownish-red at the start to a dark red in the middle and back to a brownish-red at the end. Most girls also pass dark red clots (clumps of matter) during the period. These clots are parts of the uterine wall that are being discharged.

It is not unusual to discover a few blood spots in the middle of your menstrual cycle because of ovulation. Many girls have mid-month spotting. But if you notice an unusual amount of spotting, it's a good idea to tell your mother and then, perhaps, see a doctor.

HORMONES AND YOUR PERIOD

You may wonder, "What causes my period to start and stop each month? And how does my body know to even have and continue my periods in the first place?" The answer revolves around two words—glands and hormones.

An important gland called the *pituitary gland* lies at the base of your brain. The pituitary is sometimes called the chief gland because it has two functions: to control your body's growth and maturation, and to control your menstrual cycle. The pituitary regulates these two functions by continually releasing *hormones* into your bloodstream.

The word hormone (HOR-moan) comes from a Greek word meaning "to set in motion," and hormones do just that. Hormones are chemical substances that are made in various body organs, and their function is to "set in motion" different bodily systems—such as the menstrual cycle.

Four important hormones maintain your cycle, estrogen, progesterone, FSH (follicle-stimulating hormone), and LH (luteinizing hormone). All four are involved, but the two main ones are estrogen and progesterone.

When you approach puberty your ovaries begin to make estrogen, which is a female sex hormone responsible for the many changes you encounter as you develop into an adult woman. Estrogen also plays an important role in menstruation; it is responsible for setting off the process in the uterus that causes it to thicken and to prepare for possible pregnancy.

Progesterone is another female sex hormone; it is predominantly responsible for stimulating an ample blood supply in the uterus to nourish a new life.

YOUR MONTH IN FOUR PHASES

Your period may come every 30 days. It may come every 26 or every 33 days. Regardless of when your periods come or how light or heavy your blood flow is, all menstrual cycles are alike in that they can be divided into four recurring parts, or phases.

Although you may think of your menstrual period as just the days you are having blood flow, the truth is that the entire month is involved even though you feel that nothing is going on. Actually, a lot is going on inside.

You may not feel or be affected by various monthly phases, but it is usually reassuring to know the pattern of your cycle.

Malory

"Sometimes I get my period—well, I don't get my period, but I bleed a little in the middle of the month. I couldn't figure out why until I asked my doctor and she said I was ovulating and that it was normal."

The three main changes your body goes through each and every month are:

- changes in your hormones;
- changes in your uterine lining; and
- changes in the development and movement of your egg.

If you divide the month into four distinct phases of the menstrual cycle, it is possible to pinpoint specific days for each phase. Keeping a calendar can give you a consistent idea of where you are physically and even emotionally each month.

Realize that these four phases are average time spans and are different for every female. It is an overall view of the month, so when you apply this information to your cycle, be somewhat flexible with the day count.

For the sake of this explanation, the month of November will be used to discuss the four mentrual cycle phases, with November 1 as the first day of the period. Of course, the first day of the period can start on *any* day of the month—the 1st, the 11th, the 20th, whatever. A guy I once knew thought all women in the world started their period on the first day of every month. Now that would be clockwork, wouldn't it?

PHASE 1 (YOUR PERIOD)

The first phase of your cycle begins the day your period starts and usually lasts about five days, though it may be shorter or longer.

During this time you wear sanitary protection to absorb the blood and uterine lining leaving your body. Also at this time, your hormones (estrogen and progesterone) are at their lowest levels and your egg has disintegrated. Some females feel tired and out of sorts during their periods, and this may be attributable to the low levels of hormones.

S	M	T	W	Th	F	S
		1	2	3	4	5

PHASE 2 (RIGHT AFTER YOUR PERIOD STOPS)

The second phase of your menstrual cycle usually lasts just two to four days, but important things are taking place.

During this phase your pituitary gland sends a message to your ovaries to stimulate estrogen production. Another egg in one of your ovaries begins to ripen. Meanwhile, the hormone progesterone is also being secreted in small amounts. If you could look into your uterus, you could see a thin lining beginning to develop.

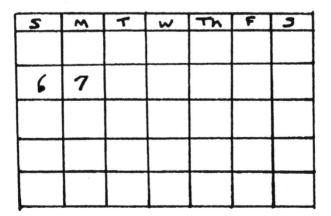

S	M	T	W	Th	F	S
6	7					

Sometimes I feel good right after my period stops. It could be because estrogen is flowing into my bloodstream once again and I'm feeling its positive effects.

PHASE 3 (THE MIDDLE OF YOUR MENSTRUAL CYCLE)

This phase begins on about the 8th day of the month and lasts about seven days.

From day 8 to about day 14 more and more estrogen is pumped into your bloodstream. On day 14 estrogen is at its highest level. At that time an egg breaks out from one of your ovaries and travels into one of your fallopian tubes. This is ovulation. Generally, your body produces only one ripe egg every month. Some scientists believe that the ovaries alternate; that is, one month the left ovary releases an egg, and the next month the right ovary releases an egg.

During this third phase progesterone is being produced to stimulate development of the uterine lining. It is at its highest level now.

The two most important days during your cycle are the day your period starts and the day you ovulate. You can

S	M	T	W	Th	F	S
		8	9	10	11	12
13	14					

never pinpoint exactly when your period will start or when you will ovulate, but you can have a very good idea. Knowing when you ovulate is important because that's the time you can become pregnant.

PHASE 4 (TWO WEEKS BEFORE YOUR PERIOD STARTS)

The fourth and last phase of your menstrual cycle occurs from about the 15th to the 28th day.

S	M	T	W	Th	F	J
		15	16	17	18	19
20	21	22	23	24	25	26
27	28					

During this phase, if fertilization has not occurred, estrogen and progesterone begin to decline. The uterine lining is quite thick during this phase and is ready to accept the implantation of a fertilized egg. If the egg is not fertilized, the uterine lining prepares to leave the body during menstruation—and you are back to Phase I.

The two weeks or so before your period starts can be stressful for some women, who experience what is called premenstrual syndrome, or PMS. Some women do not experience any negative effects up to the time their period begins. PMS is discussed further in Chapter VI.

On the calendar below mark your own menstrual cycle in four phases. Start by writing in the day your period starts, then the day it ends. Follow your entire month through, indicating specific phases as closely as you can. Try to pinpoint the day you ovulate. Did you feel any noticeable signs that this happened? Did you find a spot of blood in your underwear? If you continue to chart your cycle you will begin to see repeating patterns and will develop confidence in knowing yourself by knowing your body.

S	M	T	W	Th	F	S

If you could visualize what is taking place inside your reproductive organs during one month, it would look something like this.

Your uterus had prepared a thick, nourishing lining of blood. But your egg was not fertilized, and the lining was not needed to support the development of a baby. The uterine lining is now being released from your body through the cervix and vagina. You're having your period.

Your period just ended. Estrogen and progesterone are being secreted in small amounts, and your uterine lining is slowly building up again.

Your uterus has continued to build up its lining. Estro-

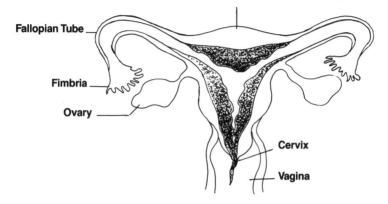

"PHASE 1"

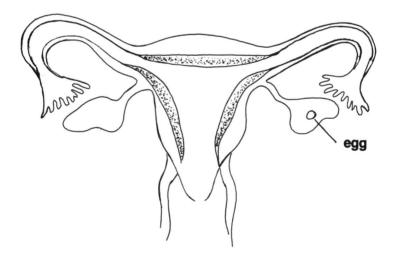

PHASE 2

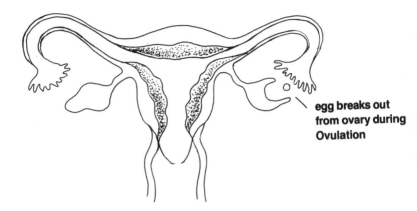

egg breaks out
from ovary during
Ovulation

PHASE 3

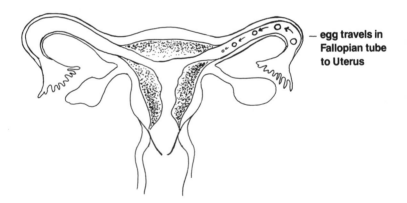

— egg travels in
Fallopian tube
to Uterus

PHASE 4

gen is at its highest level when one ripened egg bursts out from one of your ovaries.

The uterus has thickened and is ready for the implantation of a fertilized egg. The egg is moving through the fallopian tube toward the uterus. If the egg is fertilized in the tube on its journey to the uterus, it will attach to the uterus lining and grow into a baby. If the egg is not fertilized (which is what happens most often), the egg and uterine lining will be shed from the body—and you're back to Phase I, your period.

PERIODS AFFECT YOUR BODY AND MIND

Most women, although not all, feel different a few days before and during their periods. Often a wide range of subtle and not-so-subtle changes take place, and it's not uncommon to wonder if what you feel or how you feel is normal.

I've been having periods long enough so that I can practically predict how I will feel and when. For example, about a day before my period begins I usually feel very energetic. I find myself tearing my closet apart and reorganizing it. Suddenly the kitchen needs to be completely overhauled and cleaned. My car needs a good washing. Or, I have a lot of energy for sports. I can swim for a long time and seem to feel stronger. But the day my period starts, it's a whole different story. I become tired and lethargic and somewhat depressed. I usually don't have abdominal cramps, but my lower back aches for a day. My breasts used to become very tender and hurt, but for some reason that doesn't happen anymore. Sometimes my face breaks out, and I always have water retention—because I find myself consuming a lot of water. I'm thirsty! But then in a day or two, I feel back to normal, even though I still have my period.

Sometimes when we have our periods we don't realize why we feel so tense, or angry, or even elated. But those feelings are directly related to hormonal and physiological changes within us. You may find yourself in a huge argument with your sister or brother and not understand where your anger is coming from. Then the next day you get your period. Important relationships exist between your body and your mind, and if you can learn to become sensitive to your body, it will be a lot easier to understand your changing moods and emotions.

Over the years I have noticed that some of my friends don't like to admit that their periods affect them. They may call me on the phone crying, or angry. I ask, "Are you having your period?" And even if they are, they deny it. Maybe attributing depression or anger to menstruation makes some women feel out of control. Although I can understand that, I don't agree with it. To me, being in control is understanding my body and how it is affecting me physically and emotionally. That doesn't mean excusing poor behavior just because we have our periods. It means being aware of ourselves. In fact, if you feel yourself becoming irritable on the first day of your period and you are pretty sure it's because you feel "out of sorts," you are probably in a better position to control your feelings.

Let's say you just got your period. Your face has a few pimples. Your head aches. You have cramps. You feel tired. Obviously, it's not a time when you feel on top of the world and bubbling over with joy. Take time to recognize how you feel, and do things to help alleviate the distress. (More information on this is given in Chapter VI.) Figure that in a day or two you are going to feel better. This is called accepting yourself and taking charge of your life.

The following list shows some physical and mental

changes you may have during your period. Naturally, some will apply to you and many won't.

MENTAL CHANGES

Feeling:

Energetic	Vulnerable	Dizzy
Sluggish	Creative	Sad
Depressed	Out-of-it	Complete
Angry	Confused	Healthy
Sexual	Tired	Unattractive
Worried	Irritable	Picked-on
Lonely	Weak	Wanting to be alone

Physical Changes

Cramps	Mouth sores
Low back pain	Nausea
Acne/facial blemishes	Need to urinate more
Oily skin	Need to urinate less
Oily hair	Temporary weight gain
Hands, feet swell	Feeling warmer
Water retention	Stomach swells
Breasts swell, become sore	Bad breath
Diarrhea	Keener sense of smell
Constipation	Burning eyes
Cheeks look rosy	Dark circles under eyes

Appetite Changes

Craving for chocolate	Loss of appetite
Craving for sweets	Craving for red meat
Compulsive eating	Craving for salt
Thirst	Craving for seafood

I once read an article written by a man who had gone through a horrible time in his life. Although very successful, he felt his life had no meaning. His world looked grim and his future didn't offer much promise. He felt worthless to the point of wanting to take his own life. Instead, he took a laxative and soon got over a bad case of constipation. He was "relieved" and in a matter of minutes, his world looked and felt better. He was happy again.

This true anecdote tells you a great deal about how closely the body and mind work together.

WHAT DO BOYS THINK?

Boys learn about menstruation from their families, teachers, and friends. Some of them know a lot about the subject, and some know very little. Usually, however, boys are not that concerned with menstruation simply because it does not happen to them. They'll never be able to fully understand what it is like to have a period, just as you can never completely understand everything about boys.

Here are some interesting comments:

Justin: "I'm glad I don't have to deal with it, and I don't understand why it has to hurt so much sometimes."

Michael: "I'm not sure how long a girl's period lasts. I think it's about two or three days. I just don't know."

Dave: "My older brother told me it was just a natural thing. It doesn't affect me one way or the other."

Mark: "I'm glad I don't have to put up with it—and I can't understand it."

Ian: "I heard about it when I was twelve years old at sleep-away camp. I was very surprised, but I didn't think it was strange."

Rob: "I was in sixth grade and menstruation was the new 'dirty' word, so it was cool if you knew what it meant. I didn't know. It was not until my father explained the facts of life that I fully understood. I live on a chicken farm and my dad explained that the eggs we ate were actually fertilized eggs. This occurs naturally every two days for a hen and every month for a woman. That's how I learned."

Tom: "Guys don't think about it too much."

Larry: "I can always tell when my sister has her period. She gets in a really bad mood for about a day. The next day she seems like herself again."

Some girls feel embarrassed when their father finds out they have just gotten or are having their periods. Realize that your father is happy for you when you begin to develop into an adult woman. He wants you to be a healthy, happy female, and having your period is a natural part of growing up.

CATCHING THE FLOW

One of my biggest concerns when I first started having periods was figuring out how to use pads and tampons so that I was comfortable and not always worrying about blood leaking through and getting on my clothes or even irritating my skin.

Many kinds of sanitary protection are on the market, and finding the style of pad or tampon that is best for you is a smart thing to do.

Pads. If you haven't already used sanitary pads, you've probably seen them advertised in magazines, on television, or in stores. Basically, the pad is worn between your legs and is designed to absorb the blood that leaves your body. Made of layers of soft cotton, the pad is usually the first type of sanitary protection a girl uses when her periods start, but it's only one kind of menstrual protection.

It is interesting to see how sanitary protection has changed over the years and become more convenient to use.

You may wonder what women used before pads and tampons were invented. Primitive women were obliged to live in special huts for the duration of their periods. They walked on grass mats and let their blood flow on these mats, which were later burned. In other parts of the world women used "bandages" made of grass or vegetable leaves, which were also burned after use.

During the Roman Empire cloth bandages came into use. They were used over and over again and required constant laundering. In the early 1900's a softer, diaperlike pad was designed. Although this pad still had to be laundered, it was designed to fit the body more comfortably. This is the kind of pad that my grandmother, who is now over ninety years old, used for many years of her life.

It was only after World War I that disposable sanitary pads were introduced. These pads were made of cotton and used with a belt and pins.

When I first got my period my mom showed me how to use a sanitary belt and napkin. She handed me a small cardboard package containing a narrow elastic belt with hooks on the back and front to fasten to a pad. Well, the pad felt enormous between my legs and the elastic belt rubbed against my skin. I remember having the worst time fiddling with that belt and changing pads. I eventually started pinning my pads directly to my underwear, which felt better but ruined a lot of panties. I did that for years until I started using tampons. Now I'm sure I would have used the pads with adhesive strips had they been around during my teens.

These pads are made with sticky strips so that they cling directly to your underwear, requiring no belt, no pins, and no hooks. This is the type sold most frequently in public dispensers in women's washrooms.

Pads with adhesive strips come in a wide range of sizes— large, small, thick, thin. You need to experiment with different styles until you find one that's right for you. Of course, you will probably want to use a thicker pad for the first few days when your flow is heaviest, and a thinner pad when it becomes lighter.

To use this kind of sanitary pad, you just pull off the strip of paper and place the sticky side on the crotch of your

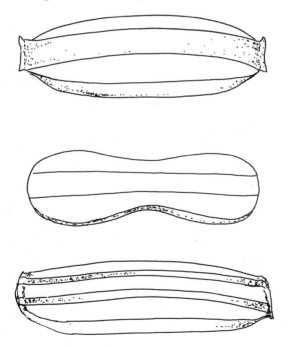

Sanitary pads come in different shapes and sizes.

underwear. The pad now lies snug to your body without slipping or moving around.

If you wear a larger pad you might worry that it would show, especially if you wear tight pants. Pad manufacturers know that females don't want their sanitary protection to show, so pads are designed *not* to show. Nevertheless, it's always a good idea to check yourself in a mirror before you go out, just to be sure.

Pads are made of soft cotton and have a plastic lining in the middle to prevent blood from leaking through to your clothing. However, if you wear a pad for too long, or if you have an unusually heavy flow, blood can leak onto the sides of your panties. Soaking the panties in cold water and then washing them should remove the discoloration.

When should you change your pad? Some girls seem to change too often, and others not often enough. I guess you have to learn your own body and judge your blood flow, changing your pad when it becomes soaked. When you are at school sitting through classes and walking around a lot, don't count on one pad lasting the entire day. Even on the days when your flow is extremely light, you would still want to change your pad.

A good rule is to change the pad every two to three hours the first couple of days of your period and then every four to five.

Another important reason for changing pads frequently is odor. Although the blood that leaves your body during menstruation is clean, once it contacts air it begins to develop an unpleasant odor because of germs. If you wear a pad too long, other people may notice this odor.

To dispose of a used pad, don't flush it down the toilet unless it is specifically designed for that. Pads can clog the plumbing. Instead, fold the pad or roll it into a ball and wrap it in toilet or tissue paper. This will help reduce odor

when you then toss it in a wastepaper basket. Public wash-rooms have metal containers next to toilets intended to hold used pads.

It's impossible to know exactly when your period will begin, but it's not impossible to be prepared. It's always smart to have extra pads or tampons in your purse or your locker at school. But if you are at school and suddenly get your period, don't be embarrassed to ask the nurse or even a teacher for a pad.

Even if you haven't had your first period yet, you may want to have a pad on hand in your purse or locker as in-surance. As mentioned earlier, a girl's menstrual flow usually begins gradually, from a whitish discharge, to a brownish discharge, and then to blood. Sometimes, however, it just begins.

In emergency, when a pad or tampon is not available, you can always fold up toilet paper, paper towels (though this would be stiff), or tissues and pin it or place it in your underwear. It won't work very well, but it's better than nothing as a temporary form of protection.

What happens if you're at school and you discover a blood stain on the back of your clothes or in your underwear? You can always keep another pair of panties handy for a quick change. You could also keep a spare pair of slacks or a skirt in your locker, though this would be trickier depending on your outfit. Remember that it's okay to tell the nurse what has happened. She may then phone one of your parents to bring you a change of clothes. Or perhaps you could just walk home, change, and then return to school. Fortunately, this doesn't happen often for most girls. But if it does happen, you just have to correct the problem and take the attitude, "So what!"

TAMPONS

Most girls use sanitary pads when they first get their periods and later also begin to use tampons. Tampons are narrow tubes of absorbent cotton designed to be inserted into the vagina.

Although tampons are not completely problem-free, they have recognizable advantages:

- When the tampon is inserted correctly into the vagina, it cannot be felt.
- No pins, pads, belts, or hooks are needed with tampons.
- Tampons are small and can easily be carried in a purse.
- Tampons can be worn while swimming.

- Tampons cannot be seen under clothing.
- As compared to pads, there is less chance of menstrual odor with tampons.
- It is not necessary to remove a tampon when using the toilet.
- Tampons are easy to use and effective.
- Tampons come in sizes for different shapes and needs.
- Tampons are sanitary because they are individually wrapped.
- Tampons can be flushed down the toilet after use.

Like the pad, the idea for the tampon is not new. For centuries, women have placed menstrual protection in the

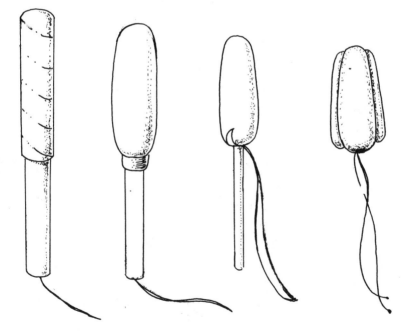

Tampons also come in different shapes and styles.

vagina. Egyptians rolled soft papyrus, Africans rolled soft grass and root and Romans wound soft wool to wear in the vagina during menstruation. In 1933 a doctor invented the first tampon to be marketed in the United States.

Basically, the tampon works because the cotton molds itself to the vagina of the user and absorbs menstrual blood. Like a sponge, the tampon becomes larger when it absorbs fluid.

Tampons can be purchased in four styles: (1) with a cardboard applicator, (2) with a plastic applicator, (3) on a stick, and (4) with no applicator or stick. There are sizes for different body shapes and menstrual flows. A "Junior" tampon is quite thin, "Regular" is medium, and "Super" or "Super-Plus" is larger.

Most women find that they use different sizes of tampons at different stages of their period. The larger tampon can be used at the start of the period when the flow is heaviest and the smaller tampon at the end when the flow is lighter.

Maybe you already use tampons. If not, you are probably interested in knowing how to use them. Before discussing how to insert the tampon into the vagina, there are some important points to cover.

Some girls worry that the tampon might "get lost" inside their body, that they might insert it and not be able to get it out. They are afraid that the tampon might work its way up into their internal organs.

First of all, it is impossible for a tampon to get into your internal organs. The tampon fits into the vagina, and that's as far as it can go. It is impossible for the tampon to get through the cervix opening, the os, which is about the size of a match head. There is no way the tampon can get into the uterus.

Second, the tampon can't "get lost" inside of you. What

may happen, however, is that the tampon string may get pushed up into the vagina. In that case you would have to reach in with your fingers and pull the tampon out.

Some girls try to use tampons before their bodies are ready. My sister, for example, struggled for hours one day determined to insert a tampon. Her vaginal opening was very small, and all the pushing and tugging caused the skin to swell. She finally did get the tampon into her vagina but then couldn't get it out. Her vaginal opening had swelled nearly shut. Mom took her to the doctor, who was able to remove the tampon.

This is an extreme example, and I mention it only because it *could* happen. If you have a great deal of trouble inserting a tampon, just wait. Your body will mature and your vaginal opening will enlarge as you get older.

Some people think that virgins can't use tampons. Using or not using tampons has nothing to do with virginity or whether you have had sexual intercourse. Yes, a virgin can use a tampon if she wants to.

The most common tampon is the kind with a cardboard applicator, and this is the style we'll discuss first. Once you get the knack of it, inserting and removing the tampon is easy. For most girls, however, the first time they try is somewhat tricky.

- Start out by using a thin, small tampon. Remove the wrapper and look at the tampon. You will see that it is encased in two cardboard tubes, one smaller than the other. The smaller tube pushes the tampon up through the larger tube and then into your vagina. The string at the end of the tampon is there so you can pull it out. First experiment with this tampon, pushing the cardboard tubes together and letting the tampon come through. Now get another tampon

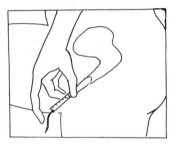
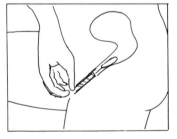
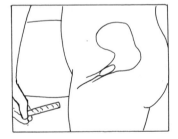

Inserting the Tampon.

and start again. *Note*: If you accidentally push the string up into the cardboard tube you can pull it back down with eyebrow tweezers.

- Take the wrapper off and hold the tampon in the hand you write with. Although you may wish to stand, sit in a chair, or sit on the toilet, I suggest lying on your bed the first time you try to insert a tampon.

  Once you are lying down, raise your knees and spread your legs slightly. Using your other hand, gently open the folds of skin around your vaginal opening. Place the tip of the tampon at your vaginal opening and push it inside just a little—about ¼ to ½ inch. When the tampon is in the opening, push the cardboard applicator. You are pushing the smaller tube into the larger tube. This causes the tampon to be pushed into your vagina. Now pull both cardboard tubes away. The tampon is in place in your vagina.

QUESTIONS

"I tried to push the tampon in, but it wouldn't go."

If you find that you can't push the tampon into your vaginal opening at all, try a little vaseline, saliva, or K–Y Jelly on the tip of the tampon. Put a little vaseline on your inner lips to moisten them so that the tampon can slip inside.

"I used some vaseline, but I still can't get the tampon in."

If you push the tampon but it does not go in, there could

be two reasons. One may be that you are pushing the tampon against the folds of your skin. You need to separate the folds so the tampon can reach your vaginal opening. The second reason may be that your vaginal opening is still too small. If this is the case, you must wait until your body matures a bit more. You could also try stretching the opening with your finger from time to time, using a little vaseline. *Note*: Don't use hand or face cream or any cream containing perfume to insert the tampon. The perfume chemicals could irritate your vaginal area and vagina.

"I got the tampon in, but it really hurts!"

When you insert the tampon correctly, you cannot feel it. If you can feel it and it hurts, you haven't pushed the tampon in far enough. It's caught at a muscle at the entrance to your vagina. This is the sphincter, a muscle that will tighten up if you are not relaxed. So calm down, relax, and try to push the tampon up farther with your finger. If you have no luck, pull it out and try again another time.

"I can get the tampon in, but it won't go any further."

When you push the tampon in, you need to angle it to the small of your back. Your vagina is angled to the small of your back; it is not straight up and down like your spinal column.

"I got the tampon in. Will it fall out?"

No. Once the tampon is in, your sphincter and the flexibility of your vagina will keep the tampon in place until you pull it out. If you have not pushed the tampon past your sphincter, it will feel as if it's falling out. You haven't inserted it correctly.

"All my friends use tampons. I've tried a million times, I follow the instructions, and no matter what I do, it won't go in!"

I understand how you feel. It took me years to be able to use tampons. I could not get the tampon in because my vaginal opening just wouldn't stretch. Then, finally, it did. But it took a lot of patience. Some girls can use tampons right away and others can't. One of my friends got her first period when her family was out at sea in a boat. The only sanitary protection her mother had was tampons, and my friend was able to use the tampon the very first time she tried. She was about thirteen then, and I couldn't use one until I was sixteen. So we're all different.

"I think my tampon's in right. How can I be sure?"

If you have inserted the tampon correctly:

- The tampon feels "right" in place.
- The tampon is past the sphincter muscle.
- You cannot feel the tampon whether you stand, sit, jump, squat, or lie down.
- The string is hanging free, outside your vaginal opening.
- The tampon is completely inside your body; you can only see the string hanging outside your vaginal opening.

Changing the Tampon.   Like using the sanitary pad, you have to judge for yourself how often to change your tampon. A safe rule is to change it about every three to four hours, or about *four times a day.* If your flow is heavy, you may have to change your tampon every couple of hours the first few days. When your period is just about over, it seems as if you could leave in one tampon for the whole day—*but don't.* Even when your flow is light, or just about over, continue to change your tampon every three or four hours—or just use a mini-pad at this time and no tampon.

"I heard that using tampons can make you sick."

In some rare instances the use of tampons has been associated with illness. A condition called toxic shock syndrome has been linked to the continuous use of tampons during menstruation—especially one type of tampon that has been taken off the market. A type of staph infection was found to be involved, causing problems such as fever, vomiting, muscle pain, diarrhea, and skin rash. The exact reason for the illness has not been fully explained. Many women use tampons all the time, and by being careful and prudent about your personal hygiene you can too. Here are some rules to follow:

- Change your tampon at least four times a day.
- Avoid wearing one tampon the entire night, or better yet, wear a pad and no tampon when you sleep.
- Try other tampon sizes than the superabsorbent ones.
- Don't forget and leave a tampon in your vagina.
- Use mini or regular pads at the start and end of your period when your flow is light.

If you are using tampons and experience fever, vomiting, diarrhea, or a rash, stop using the tampon immediately and see a doctor.

Don't forget to remove your tampons. They are so unnoticeable that it could be easy to forget you're using one. But a tampon left for too long will cause a foul odor and a vaginal discharge. And, as we discussed, other problems might occur.

Remember that it's okay to flush a used tampon down the toilet, but not the cardboard or plastic applicator.

Removing the Tampon.   All tampons are designed with a string on the end so you can pull them out. When you want to remove a tampon, gently tug on the string. With a little pulling, the tampon will slide out.

The moisture of the menstrual discharge will make the tampon expand, so that it will be larger when you remove it. Once you've taken the tampon out, flush it down the toilet.

> "I can't get it out."

If you can't seem to pull a tampon out, don't become alarmed. Normally you would remove your tampon on the toilet, but if you have trouble try lying down on the bed. Relax, and try again. Sometimes just being nervous and tense will cause the muscles of the area to tighten up.

If you are still concerned that a tampon will not come out, tell someone in your family who can help.

DOUCHING

You may have seen ads for vaginal douches or seen them for sale in drugstores or supermarkets. Douches are liquids designed to clean the vagina. They are of different

kinds, some already prepared, and some that you prepare yourself.

The vagina, like the eye, is self-cleaning. Your vagina cleans itself after your period, and it is not recommended that you use a douche. The only time you should douche is if your doctor or health practitioner suggests that you do so.

BEING ACTIVE DURING YOUR PERIOD

Some girls wonder if there are certain things you shouldn't do during your period. Should you wash your hair? Take gym class? Play sports? Go dancing? Go on dates? Eat hot or cold foods? Take a bath? Ride a horse? The answer is yes, if you feel like doing them. If you don't—don't.

CHAPTER 6

Staying Healthy, Feeling Good

Rebecca:

> "Every month it's the same thing. I start to feel crummy and then angry. It doesn't take much for me to get really mad at my younger sister and say awful things to her. The next day my period comes. My stomach has cramps and I'm so tired I can hardly get out of bed. I only wish I didn't forget my period was coming—so I could warn everyone around me."

Some girls like Rebecca dread getting their period every month. They feel sick, they feel irritable—it's a miserable time.

I know menstruation can be unpleasant at times, and although I'm glad I'm a woman and have periods—I don't eagerly wait for my next one to come. Fortunately, there are things we can do to feel and look better before and during our periods. That's what this chapter is about—

helping you to have some control over your period, rather than letting it control your life.

PREMENSTRUAL SYNDROME

Most women, although not all, experience some discomfort seven to ten days *before* their period. This discomfort, which can include symptoms such as acne, bloating, cramps, irritability, hunger, thirst, and fatigue, has been given the generic term *premenstrual syndrome*, or PMS. Fortunately, there are positive things you can do to help counteract the negative symptoms of PMS.

Have you ever complained to someone that you felt really lousy during or before your period and been told, "It's all in your head"? In other words, you were "making up" how bad you felt. "Upsets" like cramps, a bad disposition, moodiness, or fatigue are not "all in your head." In fact, they can often be attributed to your menstrual cycle.

The hormone estrogen that flows through your body might be called a "feel good" chemical. Some doctors say that estrogen is a natural antidepressant. But when the estrogen level *drops* before you get your period (which it always does), so can your good mood. Other doctors say that endorphins, other "feel good" chemicals found in the brain, also drop before your period comes. So whether it's estrogen or endorphins, or a combination of both, taking a premenstrual plunge, the result is that you may not feel your best for a few days until these chemicals begin to flow again in your body.

Is there anything you can do to fight the blues and the blahs? Yes. Following are a few suggestions that might help you feel better, and more specific problems are discussed later in the chapter.

Be active. Exercise, especially on a regular basis, has been linked to boosting endorphins in the body. This will naturally make you feel good. I know that after I swim for half an hour I'm in a better mood than when I first got into the pool. So, be active. Swim. Dance. Jog. Do aerobics. Hike. The more you move around, the better you'll feel. Also, exercise helps to reduce tension and water retention.

Try small starchy snacks. Just before your period or for the first few days of it, try snacking on carbohydrates such as oatmeal cookies, saltine crackers, or popcorn at various times throughout the day. These small treats may alleviate moodiness.

Get enough sleep. Be sure to get an adequate amount of sleep—about eight hours—at this time of the month. Feeling overtired will only add to menstrual fatigue.

Cut down on salt. Salt has a way of making the body retain water. Periods also have a way of making the body retain water. So cut down on your salt intake about two weeks to ten days *before* your period. Salt is sometimes hidden in the foods we eat. High-salt foods include diet sodas, fast foods, soy sauce, Worcestershire sauce, potato chips, and pretzels.

Do things you enjoy. Make it a point to do things that make you happy. Read, go dancing, enjoy art, exercise, cook, be with friends. Or maybe just being by yourself makes you happy. Whatever it is, find the time.

Have a healthy diet. Although we should eat healthful foods on a regular basis, it's especially important to watch what you eat before and during your period. Take a multiple vitamin daily, eat regular meals (breakfast, lunch, and dinner), and avoid too much sugar, coffee, and chocolate. Foods that are rich in vitamin B and magnesium such as green vegetables, whole grains, and nuts may be helpful in reducing the effects of PMS.

Accept yourself.   Finally, a good way to cope with the changes your body goes through before and during your period is to accept and acknowledge what's happening inside you. Remember that how you feel is not "all in your head" and that behavior changes like a temper that flares more easily or a tendency to feel like crying can and often do happen.

The above suggestions are intended to help you feel better overall. Now let's look at some specific problems and ways to counteract them. If these don't help, and you have a problem that continually causes you distress, it's vital that you see a doctor.

CRAMPS

Cramps can range from mild discomfort to severe pain. Some women have bad cramps every time they menstruate, and others have only mild cramps once in a while. Some women have cramps only when they first start to menstruate, and others don't get cramps until later on in life.

Michelle

"I'm 26 now and I usually get cramps at the beginning of my period. They hurt, but they go away in a day or so. When I started my periods when I was twelve, I *never* had cramps, and I couldn't understand what my friends were going through. Now I do."

Cramps are definitely a negative part of menstruation, and many people still are not sure what causes them. Some of the more common theories are:

- Excess blood in the pelvic area
- Poor posture
- A tipped uterus
- Poor diet
- Contractions of the uterus
- Hormone imbalance
- Constipation

Over the past twenty years scientists and doctors have discovered that cramps are related to high levels of chemicals called prostaglandins in the body during menstruation. The prostaglandins seem to cause the muscles of the uterus to "cramp up," and some women have a lot more prostaglandins than others.

Today drugs are available that are specifically designed to reduce the cramping effect of prostaglandins during menstruation. If you have trouble with cramps, it would be a good idea to discuss it with your doctor.

When I began to menstruate I had bad cramps for about a year. I remember lying on my bed doubled up in pain. If you're anything like I was, I hope the following suggestions will help reduce your cramps.

Exercise. As previously discussed, regular exercise (three times a week or more) can heighten your endorphin production and therefore help reduce cramps. Exercise will build up your back and abdominal muscles and make the entire region stronger. Specific exercises such as sit-ups and leg-lifts also strengthen the abdominal region.

Warm soothers.   By placing a heating pad or hot water bottle on your abdomen or back, you can relax the surrounding muscles for a very soothing effect. Sometimes a hot bath will do the trick, or standing in the shower and letting hot water hit your back or stomach. Remember that getting into cold water like a pool can temporarily stop your menstrual flow, whereas warm water like a hot bath can temporarily increase it.

Massage.   Massaging the lower abdomen or lower back region can alleviate cramps.

Try fish.   It's only a theory, but some evidence suggests that switching from eating red meat to fish can help counteract the production of prostaglandins. I know I often crave fish when I have my period, and maybe there's something to it. You can try it for three months or so and see if it works for you.

Pain relievers.   A number of pain-relieving drugs are on the market, and products such as Midol and Pamprin are specifically designed to reduce menstrual symptoms. These products reduce water retention because they contain low doses of diuretic chemicals such as caffeine. However, a side effect is that they can cause irritability and nervousness.

Aspirin and acetaminophen products (like Tylenol) also relieve pain from cramps, muscle aches, and breast soreness. Aspirin can be especially helpful for cramps because it counteracts prostaglandins.

If these or other products don't help, over-the-counter

drugs containing antiprostaglandins are available, but it's a good policy to check with your doctor first.

FLUID RETENTION/WATER WEIGHT GAIN

Just before your period, it is likely that you will experience fluid retention in your stomach, breasts, hands, thighs, and face. One way to get rid of this bloating is simply to get your period. Once your period starts you'll probably notice that you urinate more frequently. But there are ways to head off the monthly bloat.

Cut down on salt.   A good practice is to cut down on salt intake about halfway through your month. That means two weeks before your period stay away from salty foods (chips, pickles, fries), and cut down on adding salt to meats, eggs, salads, cottage cheese, and so on.

Exercise.   In addition to all its other benefits, exercise will help you sweat out some of the water weight gain.

Vitamin B.   Some women find that daily vitamin B (the amount found in a multivitamin/mineral supplement) can help keep bloating down. If you decide to try this, stick with about 200mg or less per day and see if it helps you.

Diuretics.   Diuretics are drugs designed to help the body rid itself of excess fluid. Although diuretics work, they have negative side effects for many people. These drugs often cause loss of potassium, which can lead to jittery, irritable feelings.

PIMPLES

Have you noticed that your skin seems to break out just before your period? This can be directly related to an increase in androgens (male hormones) that stimulate the oil glands. There are two ways to tackle the acne dilemma: preventing pimples and clearing them up.

Prevention. Chapter II offers advice on preventing pimples in the first place. In addition, if you find that your pimples seem to appear at the same spot every month (on the forehead or the chin area) before your period, think about this: Usually itchiness is a clue that a pimple is on its way. One good preventive is to apply ice wrapped in a washcloth to the itchy area for a few minutes twice a day. This will help either eliminate or diminish the pimple.

Clearing up pimples. If your skin does break out, apply a drying lotion that contains sulfur, salicylic acid, or benzoyl peroxide. Read the package instructions or ask your pharmacist for advice. Place the preparation on the pimple, let it dry, then cover it with a foundation a shade lighter than your skin color. You could try a cream cover-up designed to hide blemishes, then follow with a water-based foundation and dust on translucent powder to blend everything together. Stay away from oil-based cosmetics, which tend to aggravate blemishes.

ACHES AND PAINS

Menstruation can contribute to back, muscle, and breast pain and headaches, which are, for the most part, big "pains in the neck."

Muscle aches. Just before your period progesterone levels in your body can make you feel tired. Progesterone can also boost the production of lactic acid, a chemical that sometimes causes muscle soreness. The best bet for preventing this achy feeling is regular exercise.

Tender breasts. The reason for this soreness is fluid retention in the breasts caused by the release of estrogen and progesterone in the body. In a way, each month your breasts prepare for breast feeding as the glands and ducts enlarge and fill with fluids.

For women with large breasts, a bra that holds the breasts firmly will help ease the tenderness. As you've probably guessed, cutting down on salt will also reduce the breast fluid retention and soreness. Some women find that cutting down on chocolate and caffeine seems to reduce breast tenderness.

Backache. Uterine contractions during menstruation can give a feeling of achy pressure to the lower back. The best remedy is massaging the lower back or using a heating pad to relax the sore muscles. Antiprostaglandin drugs may also help. If these methods don't work, you can always reduce the pressure simply by lying down.

Headache. Headache seems to be a common menstrual symptom. Usually aspirin or acetaminophen (Tylenol) will bring relief, as will massage of the temples.

IRREGULAR BLEEDING

Missing periods, having frequent periods, or having an abnormal menstrual flow are all examples of irregular bleeding. Most women experience irregular bleeding at some time in their lives.

Claire

"When I got my first period I was eleven years old, and it seemed okay. Then after about three months it stopped for a whole year. I didn't know what had happened. When I started having periods again, I bled *a lot* for a while, then I became regular."

There are many reasons for irregular periods, and one is just being young. Menstruation is a new process for your body when you are an adolescent, and sometimes it takes the body months or even years to regulate itself. It is also common for adolescent girls to menstruate without ovulating. In this case, no egg ripens in the ovary, and the hormone progesterone is not produced; estrogen acts by itself, and the result may be a thick uterine lining and heavy bleeding.

Other reasons for irregular bleeding can be:

- Poor eating habits (dieting all the time, bingeing and purging, unhealthy diet, not eating enough).
- Change of environment (traveling, flying, taking a boat trip).
- Weight gain or loss.
- Emotional excitement (stress, fright, being in love, worry).
- Physical problems (health problems that a doctor should know about).
- Pregnancy.
- Alcohol/drug abuse.

Remember that most irregularities in menstruation are not serious. The time between your periods may not always be the same. Your flow may be heavy one month and light the next. You may skip your period for months at a time. (However, if you have had sexual intercourse and suspect you could be pregnant, go to a health clinic or see a doctor immediately.)

Sometimes irregular periods can indicate a health problem that needs medical attention. It's a good idea to see a doctor when:

- You have excessive bleeding such as completely soaking through a pad or tampon every hour for an entire day or two.
- You have a period that continues for more than a week with no signs of letting up. (It can be normal to menstruate for more than seven days, but signs of slowing down should be evident.)
- Your cycles are less than 18 days apart or more than 35 days apart.
- You discover spotting at times other than when you ovulate for more than three cycles. (To figure when you ovulate, count back 14 days from the first day of your bleeding. One to two days on either side of this day should indicate about when you ovulate.)
- You have severe menstrual cramps that last more than three days each month.
- You have severe cramps at other times in the month.

Most likely, if you do see a doctor you will be reassured that you are in normal health. When I was thirteen and had bad cramps and a period every 21 days, I dreaded going to my doctor. But after I found out I was okay, I was happy I had gone.

Starving, bingeing, purging.   One important reason for irregular periods is not eating right. Young women, and women of all ages for that matter, want to look nice. And sometimes looking nice is equated with looking "thin." But being too thin can have severe consequences.

Two disorders that frequently disrupt normal menstrual cycles are anorexia nervosa and bulimia. Anorexia nervosa is a dieting pattern in which the person eats less and less and is obsessed with the act of "not eating." In essence, the body is starved of energy and important nutrients and the mind is starved of the enjoyment of eating. As the person starves herself, she lives off her own body fat and muscles. Toxic (poisonous) chemicals may form as the fat and muscle tissues are used up. As the body becomes thinner and more toxic, its hormones may decrease, with the result that ovulation and menstruation may stop and other more severe problems may develop.

Bulimia is an eating disorder in which the person eats too much and then induces vomiting to get rid of the food (calories). This "have your cake and vomit it too" routine also has the potential of throwing the hormone cycle dangerously off track. In addition to the emotional and physical stress it causes, the continual inducement of vomiting can cause stomach acid to scar the esophagus and damage the teeth.

Strenuous physical training.   Women who expend a great deal of energy on a continual basis to compete in athletic events such as marathons can experience irregularity in their periods.

Ovarian cysts. A cyst is a collection of tissue or a sac of fluid that may grow anywhere in the body. Sometimes cysts grow in a woman's reproductive organs, and especially on the ovaries. Cysts can interrupt the normal menstrual cycle.

Ovarian cysts are fairly uncommon in young women. Usually they are not dangerous and either disappear by themselves or can be removed by a doctor. When you have a medical exam, a doctor will often press on your lower abdomen to check for cysts.

Cancer. Irregular bleeding is sometimes a sign of cancer, but it is important to know that the chances of cancer in a young woman are *extremely low*. Cancer may develop in the uterus, ovaries, or cervix in addition to other parts of the body. One clue to possible cancer is an *unusual amount* of blood-spotting before or after your normal period.

Having a medical exam every year is important because it gives your doctor or health practitioner a chance to make sure you don't have this problem. During the pelvic exam, which is discussed in the next chapter, a Pap test for cancer is given. All girls, including you, should have a Pap test every year. It's a simple procedure to guard your health. I've had a Pap test every year of my life since I was thirteen.

CONSTIPATION/DIARRHEA

Constipation or diarrhea or both can be triggered by changes in your menstrual cycle hormones. You may find that you become slightly constipated before your period, and when it comes you experience some diarrhea.

The solution to both problems is having ample *fiber* in

your diet such as fruits, vegetables, legumes, and cereals and breads made especially with a lot of fiber. Fiber draws more water into the bowel to help correct constipation, and it soaks up excess fluids in the bowel to help curb diarrhea. Don't go overboard, however, because eating too much fiber all at once can cause gas.

CLEANLINESS

Now that you are becoming a woman, you care about the way you look and feel more than ever. You want your hair to shine and your skin to be smooth and clear. This is good. Being healthy and taking pride in cleanliness are important at all times.

It's normal to want to smell nice. During your period or just before it you may discover that you have a kind of "fishy" odor. Before your period starts, this odor can be caused by estrogen producing mucus in your body before the blood begins to flow. Odor during the period can be caused by not changing your pad or tampon frequently enough. Once blood reaches the air, germs grow and can cause an unpleasant smell. Remember to change your pad or tampon regularly throughout the day to keep yourself clean, to reduce chafing, and to avoid odor.

Bathe daily. During your period you generally perspire more and your hair and skin are oilier. A shower or a bath will keep you clean and fresh. When you bathe, don't forget to wash your genital area with mild soap. You may have seen deodorant sprays or powders on the market designed for the genital area. Most doctors do not recommend these. Simple bathing will keep you clean. And don't forget to wear clean underwear every day—even if it means washing it by hand.

EATING RIGHT

Everything you eat or fail to eat affects your health. A good diet has many benefits such as shiny hair, clear skin, strong bones, good muscle tone, bright eyes, fresh breath, and many more. When you are an adolescent your body requires healthy food in order to grow. It's okay to have fun with food and enjoy treats, but try to be conscious of what and how you eat. Here are some important rules to go by every day.

- Eat foods from the daily food groups (milk, meat, vegetables and fruit, bread and cereal) every day.
- Eat breakfast, lunch, and dinner on a regular basis.
- Keep snacks under control.
- Don't eat a lot before going to bed.
- Stay away from "empty calories" in fast foods that can cause you to put on weight.
- Eat only moderate amounts of salt, sugar, caffeine, chocolate.
- Know when to stop eating.
- Don't starve, binge, or purge your body.
- Avoid alcohol and other drugs.
- Don't skimp on calcium foods (dairy products) and protein (meats, eggs, etc.).
- Eat fiber foods every day.
- Eating carrots can be very useful.
- Avoid greasy foods, or keep them to a minimum.
- Eat foods you enjoy; if these foods are high-calorie desserts eat them in moderation.

The accompanying chart shows what various nutrients do for you and how to get them.

What Nutrients Do for You		
Nutrient	**Function**	**Source**
PROTEIN Very important for body-building functions Poor to use as an energy source	*Builds:* Tissues, muscles, brain, hair, fingernails *Provides:* The substance so body can make hormones for normal body systems *Helps:* Fight infection *Regulates:* Body metabolism	Milk, cheese, eggs, fish, meat, soybeans, wheat germ
FATS	*Provide:* Energy *Help:* Body absorb vitamins A, D, and E; insulate and protect body organs and structures	Whole milk, cheese, butter, margarine, oils, nuts
CARBOHYDRATES If lacking, protein will be used for energy	*Provide:* Main source of body energy; brain works with help of carbohydrates *Help:* Digestion	Fruits, vegetables, whole-grain bread, cereals, grains
IRON Likely to be deficient during menstruation	The substance in blood that carries oxygen from the lungs to body cells Gives you pep	Lean meat, liver, egg yolk, green leafy vegetables, wheat germ, enriched breads and cereals, raisins

What Nutrients Do for You		
Nutrient	**Function**	**Source**
CALCIUM Likely to be low during menstruation	*Helps:* Build bones and teeth; blood clotting; nerve regulation; muscle activity; iron absorption	Whole and skim milk, cheese, green leafy vegetables, egg yolks
B VITAMINS If lacking, may feel tired, depressed, tense	*Needed for:* Steady nerves, alertness, good digestion, healthy skin and eyes, energy production	Whole-grain bread, cereals, liver, wheat germ, green leafy vegetables, lean meats, milk, peanuts, dried peas and beans
VITAMIN C Needed everyday	*Helps:* Heal sores *Needed for:* Blood clotting, iron absorption, strong teeth and bones	Citrus fruits, peppers, green leafy vegetables, tomatoes, potatoes, strawberries, cantaloupe
VITAMIN D	*Needed for:* Strong teeth and bones	Sunlight, fortified milk, fish liver oil, tunafish
VITAMIN A	*Helps:* good vision *Resists:* Night blindness, infection *Needed for:* Healthy skin, lining of eyes, nose, and lungs	Liver, milk, butter, cheese, egg yolk, dark green and yellow vegetables, carrots, oranges, apricots

WATER	Needed for a good	Drinking fountain!
6−7 glasses a day; not a nutrient, but important	water balance in body, important for tissues	

Source: *Our Bodies Ourselves*, Simon and Schuster, New York, 1973

Food cravings.   Have you ever noticed that just before your period you crave foods like candy, ice cream, crackers, or chips? Many women experience this, but giving in can cause you to put on pounds because of extra water retention; cause your skin to break out; and contribute to cramps (excess food in the intestine can push against the uterus and cause cramping).

One way to reduce these cravings is to eat three small meals and small snacks throughout the day. You won't be so tempted to eat too much. Go ahead and have a treat or two if you want, but in moderation.

CHAPTER 7

The Pelvic Exam

No matter who you are or how old you are, going to the doctor can make you feel uncomfortable. But it doesn't have to. To help you feel more relaxed about seeing a doctor or medical person for a pelvic exam, this chapter will give you lots of information about what to expect on your first visit.

First of all, many trained people in your community can give you a pelvic exam, which is a health exam designed to check a female's body on the inside and outside. Your general doctor, a health practitioner, or a gynecologist (GUYN-a-COL-a-gist) can perform this exam. A gynecologist is a doctor specifically trained to care for women's health needs.

Having a pelvic exam at least once a year is very important—like seeing a dentist once a year. Regular checkups can prevent problems and keep you feeling good about your health. Since you were young you've probably gone to doctors or have had a special family doctor. Now that you are growing up, it's more important than ever to see a medical person who is trained to deal with your physical changes and health.

GETTING READY

If it's your first time, you may want your mother or a friend to go with you. Remember to schedule your appointment when you are not having your period. The doctor will examine your internal parts, and menstruating makes it more difficult. It's also a good idea to take a shower beforehand.

BEFORE THE EXAM

When you go into the doctor's office, the receptionist will ask you to sign in. You will then be given a standard medical form to fill out. This form will go into your own chart, and it will give the doctor information about your health history. Questions about your family's health history will be asked. The doctor will also want to know when your last period was and whether you are having any problems such as irregularity. You might want to let the nurse or doctor know if this is your first pelvic exam.

Usually before the exam, a nurse will take your height and weight, check your heart, and take your blood pressure. The nurse may also chat with you about any problems you might be experiencing. You may also be asked to go to a nearby bathroom and leave a small urine sample in a container. In any case remember to go to the bathroom before the exam so you will be more comfortable.

THE EXAM

The nurse will take you to an examining room and ask you to undress and put on a paper gown or cover yourself with a sheet. The nurse will probably leave while you are undressing. It's hard to miss the examining table covered with a paper lining.

When the doctor comes in, he or she will chat for a bit and then routinely check your eyes, ears, and heart. Next the doctor will examine your breasts for any abnormal lumps. He or she will gently press on your breasts and nipples and under your arms for any signs of disease. Ask the doctor to show you how to do your own breast exam.

Now you will be asked to lie down and place your feet in the metal stirrups at the end of the examining table. This position will probably make you feel somewhat embarrassed, but it enables the doctor to look inside you and check your internal parts. Just remember that the doctor has seen many patients in this exact position. Most doctors understand, especially if it's your first time, that you feel a bit awkward.

Now the doctor will look at your genital area to make sure it's okay. After this, your internal organs will be

examined. To do this, the doctor will use a tool called a speculum (SPEK-u-lum) to hold open the vaginal walls so the doctor can see into the vaginal/cervical area.

The Pap test or Pap smear is now taken to check for cervical cancer. As stated before, this problem is very unlikely for young girls. A long cotton swab is inserted into your vagina, and cells from your cervix are gently collected. The doctor removes the swab and places the cells on a special slide, which is sent to a laboratory. During a Pap test you may feel a slight sharp sensation, or you may not.

The speculum is then removed and the doctor goes to the next step—checking to see that your uterus, cervix, fallopian tubes, and ovaries are okay. The doctor will put on rubber gloves (if not already wearing them) and place a little vaseline-like gel on the fingertips. The doctor will then put one or two fingers inside your vagina and place the other hand on your abdomen. The doctor will press your abdominal region to feel the internal organs. After this, the exam is over.

Don't hesitate to talk with your doctor about anything that's bothering you or anything you don't understand. Tell the doctor if you're having any trouble. Sometimes doctors are so busy that they need us to ask questions. But they're there to help and want to keep us healthy.

CHAPTER ◇ 8

Keep a Calendar

When you begin to menstruate, or even if you already do, buy yourself a calendar and keep it in a special place in your bedroom. Use the calendar to mark down the important days of your cycle: the day your period starts, the day it ends, and the likely day for the next one to begin.

Let's try an example. Say your period starts on the sixth of the month on a Wednesday. On your calendar make a special mark like a "P" (or whatever mark you like) on the sixth. Then, say, your period ends on the eleventh. Mark down an "E" for ended on this day. Then, starting with the sixth of the month, count forward 28 days to figure when your period will start again and mark another "P" or "P?" for that day. This way you'll have some idea of when your period will begin again.

If you have irregular periods and it's difficult to estimate a regular 28-day cycle, still mark down the days when you start, when you finish, and when you start again. Start a new calendar every year and eventually you will see your cycle becoming more regular. Keeping a calendar can help you to feel in control of your cycle and yourself. It's also helpful to keep track of your period when you need to see the doctor.

IN CONCLUSION

I hope this book has helped answer many of your questions about getting your period and growing up. I also hope that when you have other questions you will talk with people around you who can offer advice and comfort. And now that you know more about growing up, perhaps you can share some helpful advice with someone who needs it.

Remember that there will always be crummy, rotten, lousy, difficult days in our lives. There will also be plenty of wonderful days, and we owe it to ourselves to strive for happiness and good health.

Be content with who you are—there is only one "you."

Reading list

Bell, Ruth. *Changing Bodies, Changing Lives: A Book for Teens on Sex and Relationships.* New York: Random House, 1981.

Blume, Judy. *Deenie.* New York: Dell, 1974.

Gardner-Loulan, Joann; Lopez, Bonne; and Quackenbush, Maria. *Period.* San Francisco: Volcano Press, 1981.

Madaras, Lynda, with Madaras, Area. *The What's Happening to My Body? Book for Girls.* New York: Newmarket Press, 1983.

Madaras, Lynda, and Patterson, Jane. *Womancare: A Gynecological Guide to Your Body.* New York: Avon Books, 1981.

Index